*The impressive stairway to the dress circle at the Strand Theatre.*

# LONDON THEATRES
# AND CONCERT HALLS

Debra Shipley and Mary Peplow

Shire Publications Ltd

## CONTENTS

Set in 8 point Times roman and printed in Great Britain by C. I. Thomas & Sons (Haverfordwest) Ltd, Press Buildings, Merlins Bridge, Haverfordwest, Dyfed.

British Library Cataloguing in Publication Data available.

ACKNOWLEDGEMENTS
We would like to thank Mr George Hoare, former general manager of the Theatre Royal, Drury Lane, and now historian and archivist to the Stoll Moss group of theatres, for his kind help and support, and all theatre managers and staff who gave so much material for our research. All photographs in this Album are by Dominic Rotheroe.

COVER: *The interior of Drury Lane Theatre; a detail from a Victorian engraving.*

# LIST OF THEATRES

*Page numbers in italic refer to illustrations*

*The handsome vestibule of the Criterion Theatre reflected in the mirror which points the way down to the theatre.*

# INTRODUCTION

The history of theatres in Britain begins in the sixteenth century. Elizabethan London was still essentially a medieval city filled with a whole host of entertainments. Pageants and processions brought colour to the streets and to the river Thames, tournaments were held at Smithfield and athletic events at Finsbury Fields. Fairs were regular and popular, with a variety of entertainers such as acrobats, tumblers and contortionists.

Professional actors performed in the open on trestle stages but by the middle of the sixteenth century plays had become so popular that some inns were used as theatres, accommodating the trestle at one end of the yard. Official disapproval of the performance of plays led to the first purpose-built theatre being situated outside the city boundaries. In 1576 John Brayne financed, and James Burbage built, the first public playhouse in London for use of a company of professional players. It was half a mile outside the city, in Shoreditch. Burbage named it simply 'the Theatre'. A year later he opened a second theatre in Shoreditch called the Curtain (after the piece of land it was built on). In 1597, when the lease on the Theatre was due to expire, it was decided to move the whole building from its Shoreditch site to Bankside where it opened in the autumn of 1598, renamed the Globe Theatre. It became the most famous of all London theatres; many of

William Shakespeare's plays were performed there. Meanwhile, in 1587 the Rose Theatre, and in 1594 the Swan were built, followed by the Fortune and the Hope. Only the Globe and the Fortune survived to the 1640s when Oliver Cromwell closed all theatres by Act of Parliament.

After the restoration of Charles II in 1660, the theatre quickly revived and in 1661 William Davenant opened the Lincoln's Inn Fields theatre (a converted tennis court), the first theatre to have a proscenium arch and set scenery. Thomas Killigrew opened the Theatre Royal, Bridges Street (Drury Lane) in 1663. Both theatres had Letters Patent of Charles II which granted the exclusive right to present legitimate drama. This was very frustrating for ambitious professionals such as Samuel Foote who in 1766 finally gained a limited patent for the Little Theatre in the Hay (Haymarket), which had opened in 1720, to put on plays for the summer months only. John Rich owned the Lincoln's Inn Fields theatre. In 1732 he built the Theatre Royal, Covent Garden and transferred the patent to the new theatre. Apart from Sadler's Wells, which had opened as a 'Musick House' by 1683, only these theatres have survived to the present and all have been rebuilt. Most of the theatres in this book opened in the great period of theatre building in London between 1866 and 1936 when eighty new theatres were

3

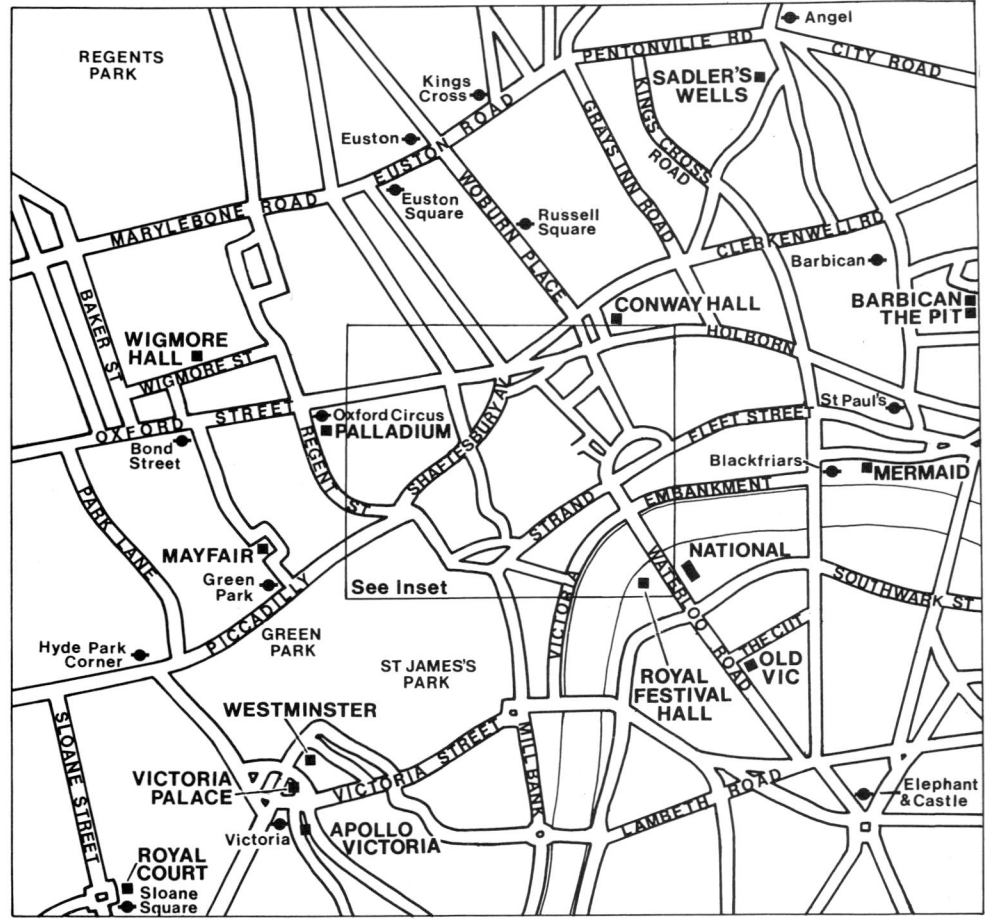

*Map of London theatres.*

built.

In 1675 what was probably the first public concert in Europe, for which he charged one shilling admission, was staged by John Banister, the former director of King Charles II's twenty-four violins, in his newly-formed music school in Whitefriars. He was quickly followed by Thomas Britton, a charcoal merchant who from 1678 to 1714 held weekly concerts in the specially converted loft over his coalhouse in Clerkenwell. These were not grand or momentous beginnings because most of the people who knew enough to appreciate other than folk or popular music were, and remained for a long time, the royal, aristocratic and wealthy who commissioned the music, employed the musicians and held private concerts.

The audience began to expand through subscription concerts for which admission to a series of concerts was subscribed in advance. Concert halls such as the Hanover Square Rooms and the Argyll Rooms were small by modern standards. From the beginning of the nineteenth century the formation of the first orchestral society (the Philharmonic, 1813) and many choral societies reflected a widening interest, particularly in the large-scale orchestral works and oratorios. The public filled large halls such as the Exeter Hall (now the Strand Palace Hotel) built in 1831, and the St James's Hall (where the Piccadilly Hotel now stands) built in 1838. When choruses of 700 voices were assembled week after week to sing oratorios in the Crystal Palace (1851) thousands flocked to hear them. In such a climate the Royal Albert Hall (1870) was built and audiences keen to hear great music went to the Queen's Hall Promenade Concerts from 1893. Only the Albert Hall survives of the great nineteenth-century halls, but it is perhaps sufficient: sophisticated modern audiences enjoy a wider range of music of which only a tiny proportion needs such a vast auditorium.

---

A box office telephone number is given for each theatre. For performances the same day the Society of West End Theatres (telephone 01-836 0971) also runs a ticket booth in Leicester Square which opens at midday for matinee tickets and from 2.30 p.m. to 6.30 p.m. for evening performances. A maximum of four tickets per person can be bought for half the normal seat price plus a small service charge, for cash only. The Theatres Trust was set up by Act of Parliament 'for the better protection of theatres for the benefit of the nation'. For information about the work of the trust write to 10 St Martin's Court, St Martin's Lane, London WC2N 4AJ. Telephone: 01-836 8591.

*Theatres in the central London area.*

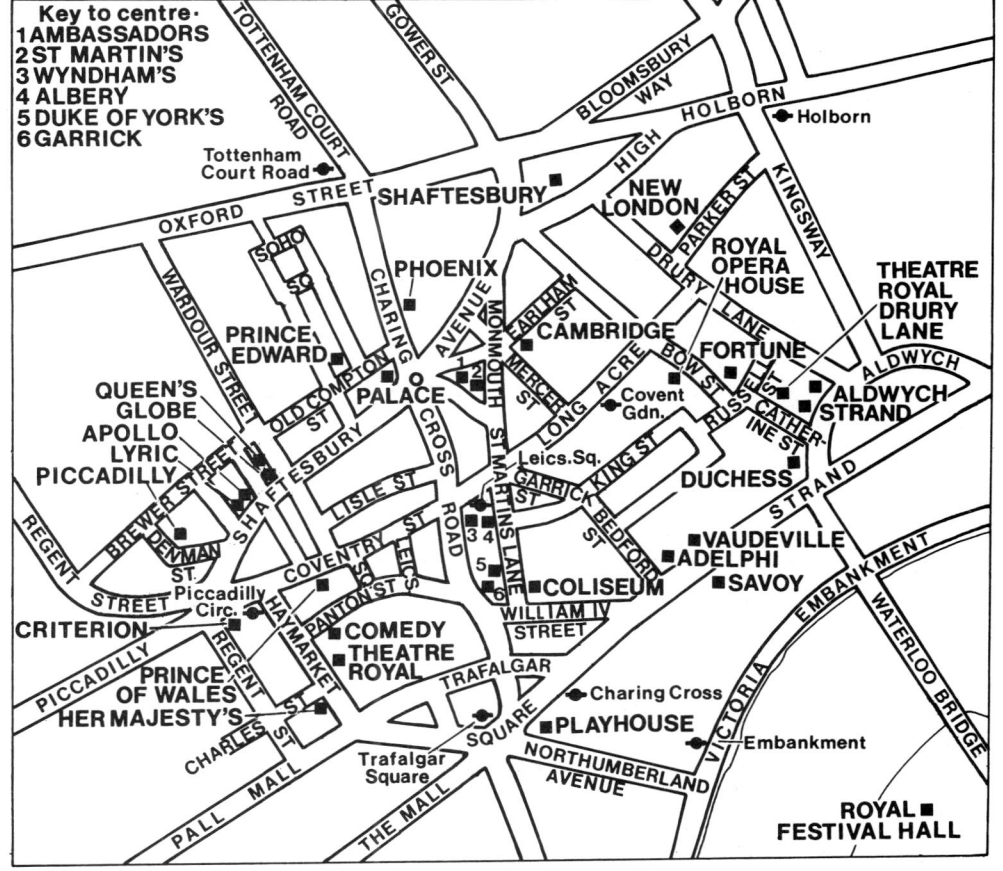

# THEATRES AND CONCERT HALLS

## Adelphi Theatre

Strand, WC2E 7NA.
Box office telephone: 01-836 7611.
1500 seats.

Theatres on this site since 1806 have been called the Sans Pareil (1806), the Adelphi (1819 and 1942), Theatre Royal, Adelphi (1829 and 1858), Royal Adelphi Theatre (1867 and 1902) and the Century (1901). During that time the building was once demolished and three times reconstructed. The present building retains the nineteenth-century outer walls and the Royal Entrance. In 1834 the first mechanical sinking stage in Britain was installed. From 1837 to 1845 the first adaptations of Dickens' novels were seen here, followed by the popular Adelphi dramas and later by the Adelphi melodramas starring William Terriss whose fate eclipsed his roles when he was assassinated at the stage door in 1897.

Since 1901 the Adelphi has presented many

*The stage door and the Royal Entrance to the Adelphi Theatre.*

successful musicals, starting with *The Quaker Girl* in 1908. Gladys Cooper starred in *Peter Pan* in 1923 and Jessie Matthews in Rodgers and Hart's *Evergreen* in 1930 which opened the present building designed by Ernest Shaufelberg. Memorable later productions include Marie Tempest's last London appearance in *Dear Octopus* (1938), Ivor Novello's *The Dancing Years* (1942), five shows by A. P. Herbert and Vivian Ellis (1947-9), Beatrice Lillie in *Auntie Mame* (1958), Van Johnson in *The Music Man* (1961), *Charlie Girl* with Anna Neagle (1965, 2,200 performances) and the revival of *Me and My Girl* (1985).

## Albery Theatre

St Martin's Lane, WC2N 4AH.
Box office telephone: 01-836 3878.
876 seats.

Having built Wyndham's in 1899, Sir Charles Wyndham and his wife Mary Moore built a theatre on land adjoining, which opened as the New Theatre in March 1903. After Wyndham's death the theatre was managed by Bronson Albery, Mary Moore's son by a former marriage, in whose honour the theatre was renamed in 1973. It is now managed by his grandson. The theatre was the thirtieth designed by architect W. G. R. Sprague. The interior was designed by Claude Ponsonby and has changed little since it was described in 1903 as 'exquisite ... of the period of Louis XVI ... adhered to even down to the minutest details throughout'.

Sir Charles and Miss Moore starred in the opening play *Rosemary*. Noël Coward's first produced play opened in 1920 and in 1924 Sybil Thorndyke surpassed previous appearances here in the first London production of Shaw's *St Joan*. In 1927-8 the *Constant Nymph* by Margaret Kennedy ran for 587 performances during which John Gielgud's association with the theatre as actor and producer began. His productions of Gorden Daviot's *Richard of Bordeaux* (1933) and *Hamlet* (1935) were particularly notable. During the Second World War and after the Albery was the temporary home of the companies of Sadler's Wells (until 1944) and the Old Vic (until 1950). Outstanding productions starred Laurence Olivier in *Richard III* and Ralph Richardson in *Henry IV, Parts I and II*. T. S. Eliot's *The Cocktail Party* followed the Old Vic's departure and among many later successes were Ray Lawler's *Summer of the Seventeenth Doll* (1957), Dylan Thomas's *Under Milk Wood* (1956),

Lionel Bart's record-breaking musical *Oliver* (1960-6) and the Tim Rice/Lloyd Webber musical *Joseph and the Amazing Technicolour Dreamcoat* (1973).

# Aldwych Theatre

Aldwych, WC2B 4DF.
Box office telephone: 01-836 6404.
1092 seats.

W. G. R. Sprague built the Aldwych and the Waldorf (now the Strand theatre) in 1905 to flank his French chateau-style Waldorf Hotel (1907). It was built for Seymour Hicks and impresario Charles Frohman but it was not until 1923 that the success of the farce *Tons of Money* with Tom Walls and Ralph Lynn started a succession, until 1933, of plays by Ben Travers dubbed the 'Aldwych farces'. *Cuckoo in the Nest* (1925) was the first.

Notable productions include Tennessee Williams's *A Streetcar Named Desire* (1949) with Vivien Leigh and Christopher Fry's *The Dark is Light Enough* (1954). From 1960 to 1982 the Royal Shakespeare Company made its London home here presenting a fascinating range of productions from *Marat/Sade* by Peter Weiss (1964) and Peter Nichols's *Privates on Parade* (1977) to the *The Greeks* by Euripides and John Burton (1980) and the musical version of *Nicholas Nickleby* (1980). The alterations to the interior made by the RSC have since been restored.

# Ambassadors Theatre

West Street, Cambridge Circus, WC2H 9ND.
Box office telephone: 01-836 6111.
460 seats.

Another handsome theatre designed by W. G. R. Sprague in Louis XVI style, the Ambassadors opened in 1913. Ambassadorial crests were part of the original design which included a colour scheme of Parma violet, ivory and dull gold. It was very handsome and apart from some reseating and redecoration the theatre has been little altered.

Inevitably the modern view of the Ambassadors is dominated by the phenomenal twenty-one year run of Agatha Christie's *The Mousetrap* from 1952 to 1974 (after which it transferred to the St Martin's). The theatre owed its first success to C. B. Cochrane who presented Alice Delysia in a series of revues beginning with *Odds and Ends* in 1914. During H. M. Harwood's lease of the theatre from 1919 to 1930 Ivor Novello made his debut in *Deburau* (1921) and Paul Robeson made his first London appearance in *The Emperor Jones* (1925).

*Theatre signs light up West Street, Cambridge Circus.*

Vivien Leigh made her debut in Carl Sternheim's *The Mask of Virtue* in 1932. From 1939 to 1947 intimate revues, mainly by Alan Melville and starring Hermione Gingold and Henry Kendall, were very successful, ending with *Sweetest and Lowest* (1946).

# Apollo Theatre

Shaftesbury Avenue, W1V 7HD.
Box office telephone: 01-437 2663.
769 seats.

The Apollo stands in a row of four theatres and is, architecturally, strikingly different. Opened in 1901, the fourth theatre in Shaftesbury Avenue, it was built for Henry Lowenfeld to the designs of Lewen Sharp. The facade is in French renaissance style with winged figures adorning the rounded ends of the top storey. At one time it was thought Lowenfeld might call his new theatre the Mascot as a feature of the decoration was the theatre's lucky mascot, a silver chain and buckle with a flying lizard supported by rampant lions, an

7

original badge of the German tribe of gypsies with whom the Lowenfeld family were connected.

Designed for musicals, the opening show *The Belle of Bohemia* was a disappointment but *Kitty Grey* (1902) was the first of a successful series of George Edwards musicals. The original production of *Tom Jones* (1907) featured Cicely Courtneidge. Harold Brighouse's *Hobson's Choice* was an immediate success in 1916 and after Ian Hay's *Tilly of Bloomsbury* (1919) the theatre was set on its almost consistent course of success. Memorable productions include Elizabeth Bergner in *Escape Me Never* (1933), Patrick Hamilton's *Gaslight* (1939), Rattigan's *Flarepath* (1942-4), *Seagulls over Sorrento* (1950), *Boeing-Boeing* (1962-5), John Gielgud in Alan Bennett's *Forty Years On* (1968) and, with Ralph Richardson, *Home* (1970), and Alan Ayckbourne's *The Norman Conquests* (1975).

# Apollo Victoria

Wilton Road, SW1V 1LL.
Box office telephone: 01-828 8665.
1544 seats (2572 maximum).

The Apollo Victoria was built in 1930 as the New Victoria Cinema, one of the ultra-modern super-cinemas of the time. It opened as a theatre in February 1980, specially redesigned for presenting full scale musicals, and has since staged *The Sound of Music* starring Petula Clark in 1981-2, *Fiddler on the Roof* in 1983 and *Starlight Express* which began its run in 1983. There have also been pop concerts here with international stars such as Shirley Bassey, Sammy Davis Junior and Cliff Richard.

The original blue and green interior has been redecorated in pink, gold and white but still retains many of the original 1930s' decorative features. The Apollo has become a favourite with both players and audiences, the unobstructed view combining with advanced technical facilities to give tremendous scope for imaginative stage design and innovative performances.

# Barbican Centre

Silk Street, EC2Y 8DS.
Box office telephone: 01-628 8759/638 8891.
Barbican Concert Hall, 2026 seats; Barbican Theatre, 1162 seats; The Pit, 150-280 seats.

The Barbican Centre, opened in 1982, is the largest arts complex of its kind in Europe, situated close to the old Roman and medieval walls of the City of London (a barbican is the outer defence of a city or castle). The **Barbican Concert Hall** is the home of the London Symphony Orchestra and doubles as a conference centre; the **Barbican Theatre,** remarkable for its comfort and the unusual automatically

*The Lakeside Terrace at the Barbican Centre.*

closing doors at the end of each seat row, is the London base for the Royal Shakespeare Company; **The Pit** is a small intimate space.

The Barbican also contains three cinemas, each fully equipped for conferences, and five seminar rooms. There is an art gallery with a permanent collection and space for visiting exhibitions. The enormous foyer space on several levels is also used for displays and exhibitions and for informal musical entertainments at lunchtime and in the early evening. There are bars, buffets and two restaurants, the most popular being on the Lakeside Terrace where visitors sit and watch the fountains in the summer.

The Centre is signposted for people arriving on foot, by public transport and by car — there are 500 parking spaces in the Centre and 1200 nearby, including a 24-hour car park in Aldersgate Street.

# Cambridge Theatre

Earlham Street, WC2 9HU.
1275 seats.

The Cambridge was one of the three new theatres which opened in September 1930 and the one which made no concessions in the modernity of its architecture and especially its interior design, which was described as 'beautiful, if peculiar', 'Teutonic' and 'futuristic' by the *Stage*.

It opened on 4th September with Beatrice Lillie in *Charlot's Masquerade*. Later, under Jay Pomeroy, the theatre housed excellent opera productions, mainly revivals, and foreign ballet companies. Pomeroy founded the New London Opera Company at the Cambridge and Menotti's opera *The Consul* was first heard here in 1951.

In 1952 drama returned and during the next few years the theatre had successes with long runs of *The Reluctant Debutante* (1955), *Billy Liar* (1960-2), and Tommy Steele in *Half a Sixpence* (1963), based on H. G. Wells's *Kipps*. In spite of a series of transfers and repertory productions by the National and other theatre companies the theatre closed in 1980, not to reopen until 1987/8.

# (London) Coliseum

St Martin's Lane, WC2N 4ES.
Box office telephone: 01-836 3161.
2358 seats.

Since 1968 the home of the Sadler's Wells Opera (now the English National Opera), the Coliseum is a large and cheerfully brash

*The Coliseum, home of the English National Opera company.*

building. When it opened in 1904 the owner Oswald Stoll intended it to be, and the designer Frank Matcham ensured that it was, the largest, best equipped and most impressive theatre in London. A contemporary account of 'London's new pleasure-house' extolled its virtues with some awe, including 'waiting rooms with the free use of telephones and shorthand typists as well as a fine restaurant where a band will play between shows'. In its first week over 67,000 people flocked to wonder at this monument to the extravagance of the Edwardian era. It was the first theatre in England to have a revolving stage (with three separate revolves) and the first in Europe to have lifts installed. It is still the largest theatre in London.

Between 1909 and 1931 the Coliseum was mainly a music hall, although many famous actors featured on the bill including Ellen Terry, Edith Evans, Lillie Langtry and Sarah Bernhardt. As interest in the music hall declined, revues and musical comedies were featured as well as dance productions. Diaghilev's Russian Ballet performed here in

1918 and 1924. After 1931 Stoll set out to create the most lavish productions in London. *White Horse Inn* (1931) ran for 651 performances but other productions were less successful. Closed from 1939 to 1945, American musicals provided popular postwar runs starting with *Annie Get Your Gun* (1947).

The final rejuvenation was provided when it was modernised in 1968 and became the national centre for opera sung in English. The Sadler's Wells Opera (which became the English National Opera Company in 1974) at last took over a stage and auditorium suitable for grand productions such as Wagner's *Ring of the Nibelungs*, first presented in 1973. Today it presents opera and ballet throughout the year.

# Comedy Theatre

Panton Street, SW1Y 4DN.
Box office telephone: 01-930 2578/9.
820 seats.

During the nineteenth century, Panton Street was an unsavoury area filled with 'night

*A statue on the facade of the Comedy Theatre.*

houses' of dubious reputation and was perhaps an unusual place to build, in the remarkably short period of six months, a new theatre. Designed by Thomas Verity, the Royal Comedy Theatre opened in 1881 to instant approval for *The Mascott*, a comic opera by Audan. Two wellwishers attending the first performance were the Prince and Princess of Wales and such patronage ensured a prosperous start for the new theatre. The interior was fitted out in renaissance style, richly moulded and finished in white and gold. The 'Royal' prefix was dropped in 1884. Alterations were made in 1893, 1903 and 1933, but the structure remained original until 1954 when it underwent major reconstruction to meet modern requirements. In 1981, the theatre was redecorated in the present gold and red, in honour of its centenary year.

Diversity has been the keynote of productions since the theatre opened. *Monsieur Beaucaire* was a great success in 1902, John Barrymore made his first London appearance here in 1905 and Marie Tempest appeared from 1907 to 1909. Revues filled the theatre from 1915 to 1919 and again in the 1930s.

In 1956 the New Watergate Theatre Club was formed to enable audiences to see controversial plays and staged Arthur Miller's *A View from the Bridge* (1956), Robert Anderson's *Tea and Sympathy* (1957), Tennessee Williams's *Cat on a Hot Tin Roof* (1958) and Peter Shaffer's *Five Finger Exercise* (1959). The New Watergate Theatre Club played an important role in changing the view of censorship which eventually led to its abolition in 1968.

More recent successes include Peter Nichols's *A Day in the Death of Joe Egg* (1967), the transfer of *There's a Girl in my Soup* (1969, 2547 performances), Nell Dunn's *Steaming* (1981) and *Little Shop of Horrors* (1984).

# Conway Hall

Red Lion Square, WC1.
Box office telephone: 01-242 8032/3.
500 seats; small hall 100.

Conway Hall, built in 1929 for the South Place Ethical Society, a humanist educational charity, is named after Moncure Conway, a pioneer of the intellectual revolution which took place during the nineteenth century. The society has, since 1887, worked towards 'increasing the popularity of good music by means of cheap concerts'; a principle which is maintained today, making it an attractive venue particularly for pensioners and students who patronise its wide range of classical music concerts.

# Criterion Theatre

Piccadilly Circus, W1V 9LB.
Box office telephone: 01-930 3216.
606 seats.

The Criterion is London's only theatre built entirely underground — only the main entrance and vestibule are on ground level. One of the best works of Thomas Verity, it was built below the Criterion restaurant and opened in 1874. Apart from some redecoration the handsome auditorium is much as it was after it was modified (to meet safety requirements) in 1884 and is probably one of the most completely preserved in London.

With Charles Wyndham as lessee and manager until 1899, the Criterion began to establish a reputation for urbane comedy, light drama and sophisticated revue. Marie Tempest appeared in five plays between 1926 and 1929 and Terence Rattigan's *French Without Tears* ran for 1039 performances (1936-9) after which the theatre became a BBC sound studio for the duration of the Second World War. It reopened in 1945 with *The Rivals* with Edith Evans as Mrs Malaprop. A long list of later successes includes Samuel Beckett's *Waiting for Godot* (1955) which influenced much modern drama, Iris Murdoch's *A Severed Head* (1963), Joe Orton's *Loot* (1966), Simon Gray's *Butley* (1971), Alan Ayckbourne's *Absurd Person Singular* (1973) and Ray Cooney's *Run for your Wife* (1982, and still running in 1987).

ABOVE: *The Conway Hall.*
BELOW: *The ornate entrance to the Criterion Theatre, surmounted by a mask of comedy.*

*The Duke of York's Theatre.*

# Duchess Theatre

Catherine Street, Covent Garden, WC2B 5LA.
Box office telephone: 01-836 8243.
487 seats.

Built in 1929 by Ewan Barr and one of the smallest and most congenial theatres in London, the Duchess swiftly recovered from a production which never finished its first night in 1930 and went on to provide a broad range of successful productions. J. B. Priestley produced two of his plays here, *Eden End* (1934) and *Cornelius* (1934), and Emlyn Williams appeared in two of his, *Night Must Fall* (1935) and *The Corn is Green* (1938-9). T. S. Eliot's *Murder in the Cathedral* (1936), Coward's *Blithe Spirit* (1942) and Rattigan's *The Deep Blue Sea* (1952) were later successes but all previous productions were eclipsed in popularity by the nude show *Oh Calcutta!* which ran for 3918 performances (1974-80). *No Sex Please, We're British!* transferred from the Garrick in 1987 and finished here in the same year, after seventeen years in the West End.

# Duke of York's Theatre

St Martin's Lane, WC2N 4BG.
Box office telephone: 01-836 5122.
649 seats.

Owned since 1978 by Capital Radio, London's largest commercial radio station, the Duke of York's presents straight drama, shows and live pop concerts, which are staged and recorded by Capital, continuing a trend in its history towards adaptability and a wide variety of entertainment: it has staged opera, revue, ballet, musicals and even fashion shows.

From its opening in 1892 as the Trafalgar Square Theatre (renamed in 1895) the Duke of York's was a success. Its first hit, in 1896, was *The Gay Parisienne* and from 1902 to 1908 *The Admirable Crichton, Peter Pan* and other plays by J. M. Barrie had their first productions here. Noël Coward's revues *London Calling* (1923) and *Easy Virtue* (1926) were followed later by Peggy Ashcroft's memorable performance in *Jew Süss* (1929). Damaged during the Second World War the theatre reopened in 1943 and has since housed a number of notable productions including Hugh Mill's *The House by the Lake* (1956) with Flora Robson, Frank Marcus's *The Killing of Sister George* (1956), Alan Ayckbourne's first London hit, *Relatively Speaking* (1967), Tom Kempinski's *Duet for One* (1980) and Richard Harris's *Stepping Out* (1984).

The fine plasterwork of the interior has been renovated by Robin Beynon and refurbished in the spirit of the original architect's concept. The result would perhaps be recognised by the theatre's first owner, Violet Melnotte, who is said to remain as its resident ghost.

# Fortune Theatre

Russell Street, WC2B 5HA.
Box office telephone: 01-836 2238.
440 seats.

The theatre Lawrence Cowen squeezed in next to a church in 1924 was supposed to be called the Crown, but ended up as the Fortune and opened with a production of Cowen's *The Sinners,* equally appropriate to its neighbour. The bronze 'Nude Girl' on the facade, by the architect Ernest Shaufelberg, was perhaps less so. John Wall's production of Frederick Lonsdale's *On Approval* (1927) was almost the only success before it was given over to amateur companies and then to ENSA during the Second World War. But the intimate atmosphere produced by the narrow auditorium was ideal for *Joyce Grenfell Requests the Pleasure* (1954) as well as for *At the Drop of a Hat* (1957) with Flanders and Swann which ran for 733 performances. Alan Bennett, Peter Cook, Dudley Moore and Jonathan Miller made their names and media history here in 1961 with *Beyond the Fringe* which ran for 1184 performances. Despite memorable productions such as *The Promise* (1967) with Judi Dench and Ian McKellen the future was not assured and the theatre was threatened with redevelopment and closed for a short time in 1982. It reopened with *Mr Cinders* in 1983.

# Garrick Theatre

Charing Cross Road, WC2H 0HH.
Box office telephone: 01-836 4601/2.
656 seats.

The long neo-classical Portland and Bath stone facade of this late Victorian theatre is a striking feature of the southern end of Charing Cross Road. Designed by Walter Emden and C. J. Phipps for W. S. Gilbert, the Garrick opened in April 1889, although two years before building work had very nearly been abandoned halfway through. The deep excavations needed for the below-ground auditorium unearthed a river which flooded the foundations and Gilbert said he contemplated letting the fishing rights rather than going ahead with the theatre!

Mrs Patrick Campbell as *The Notorious Mrs Ebbsmith* (1895) created a sensation which was further enhanced when a woman called Ebbsmith drowned in the Thames with a ticket for the play in her pocket. Arthur Bourchier who ran the theatre from 1900 to 1915 is celebrated for his excellent productions and for refusing to admit A. B. Walkley, drama critic of *The Times,* to the theatre. Bourchier's ghost is said to walk the theatre.

During the early 1930s there were plans to turn the ailing Garrick into a cinema. However, fortunes were revived in 1935 with Walter

*The Fortune Theatre.*

13

*The neo-classical Garrick Theatre was designed for W. S. Gilbert.*

Greenwood's *Love on the Dole* which brought stardom to Wendy Hiller. Devoted mainly to revue until after the Second World War, the theatre has since had consistent success with comedy, ranging from the dramatic, such as Charles Dyer's *Rattle of a Simple Man* (1962) to the farces staged by Brian Rix in 1967-71 starting with Ray Cooney and Tony Hilton's *Stand by your Bedouin. No Sex Please, We're British* broke all records in its run from 1982 to 1987.

The Italian renaissance style interior is almost unaltered and much of the original plaster decoration remains. The box front of the dress circle tier is decorated with groups of cupids carrying shields crowned with laurels. On each shield is written the name of a famous author.

# Globe Theatre

Shaftesbury Avenue, W1V 8AR.
Box office telephone: 01-437 3667.
897 seats.

Built by W. G. R. Sprague, behind the handsome stone facade the Globe has a splendid Louis XVI style interior with an impressive cupola (which is quite coincidental as the theatre opened as the Hicks in 1906 and was renamed in 1909). It has been controlled by some of the most eminent managers, starting with Charles Frohman and including Anthony Prinsep and H. M. Tennent. Early in its history the Globe braved theatrical superstition by producing *The Clock Goes Round*, a play with thirteen characters, one of whom carried a fan of peacock feathers and wore a green dress. Superstition triumphed: the play ran for just thirteen performances. In 1927 the Globe took a different sort of risk for the time with a production of *Potiphar's Wife* in which Jeanne de Casalis appeared on stage in pyjamas.

There have been many notable productions including Christopher Fry's adaptation of Jean Anouilh's *Ring Around the Moon* (1950) in which Paul Scofield made his mark, Graham Green's *The Complaisant Lover* (1959), Robert Bolt's *A Man for all Seasons* (1960), Peter Shaffer's *The Private Ear* and *The Public Eye* (1962), the long run of *There's a Girl in my Soup* (1966, 1321 performances), several plays by Alan Ayckbourne and the award-winning *Daisy Pulls it Off* (1983).

# Her Majesty's Theatre

Haymarket, SW1Y 4QR.
Box office telephone: 01-930 4025.
1264 seats.

Architect and playwright, Sir John Vanbrugh, who built the first theatre here, named it the Queen's after Queen Anne. It opened in April 1705 with the celebrated beauty Lady Sutherland in *The Lovers of Ergasto* by Giacomo Greber, but within a few years it proved to be much more suitable for opera, which the newly-arrived Handel was trying to introduce to England. From 1711 to 1739 many of his operas were produced here as well as the first oratorio to be heard in England, *Esther* (1732). As the Italian Opera House, as it became known, the theatre was continuously successful, surviving rebuilding following a fire in 1789 and changes of name according to the sex of the monarch — from King's it became Her Majesty's on the accession of Queen Victoria in 1837. After the fire of 1867, however, it did not reopen until 1877 and had so little success that it closed in 1891 and was demolished.

The present magnificent French renaissance-style theatre was built by C. J. Phipps for Beerbohm Tree in 1897 and the dramatic successes of the next eighteen years were followed on Tree's departure by the amazing 2238 performances of the musical *Chu Chin Chow* from 1916. Since then Her Majesty's has managed to present plays and musicals with equal success, some of the more notable being Noël Coward's *Bitter Sweet* (1929), George Robey as Falstaff in *Henry IV, Part I* (1935), Robert Morley's *Edward, My Son* (1947), *Brigadoon* (1949), *West Side Story* (1958), Topol in *Fiddler on the Roof* (1967), Peter Shaffer's *Amadeus* (1981) and *Phantom of the Opera* (1986).

While Tree was at Her Majesty's he formed a drama school which was eventually moved from the theatre to become the Royal Academy of Dramatic Art.

# London Palladium

Argyll Street W1A 3AB.
Box office telephone: 01-437 7373.
2317 seats.

The theatre opened on Boxing Day 1910 as the Palladium (it was renamed the London Palladium in 1934). Opened at the height of the variety and music hall boom, it was intended to rival the Hippodrome and Col-

*Her Majesty's Theatre in Haymarket was built for Beerbohm Tree.*

iseum in magnificence and size (only the Coliseum now has more seats).

The basis for the facade of the present day theatre with its classical temple front adorned with Corinthian columns was the Corinthian Bazaar of the 1860s. In 1871 Frederick Charles Hengler, a circus showman, took over the building as a permanent home for his touring circus, Hengler's Grand Cirque. The present day safety curtain gives some idea of how the building looked in those days. When the circus eventually lost its popularity after some twenty years, it was reopened as the National Skating Palace with a rink of real ice. It was then converted to a music-hall and opened with a variety bill which included Nellie Wallace, Whit Cunliffe, Ella Retford and Ella Shields, but the star of the first night was the building itself. Designed by Frank Matcham in French rococo style, it was generally agreed to be the last word in luxury with a palm court at the back of the stalls where a ladies' orchestra played between performances and, a special feature, box-to-box telephones. The theatre still retains the richly ornate decor of the variety palace heyday with most of the original ornament in the bars and foyer.

The variety boom lasted until the early 1920s, after which spectacle became popular. In 1922, Harry Day's great spectacle *Rockets* ran for nearly 500 performances. This was followed by *Whirl of the World* starring a new comedian, Tommy Handley. Throughout the 1930s the Palladium presented a series of *Crazy Gang* shows, with Flanagan and Allen, Nervo and Knox, Naughton and Gold and 'Monsewer' Eddie Gray. The Palladium was the home of *Peter Pan* every Christmas from 1930 to 1938 with 'Peters' who included Jean Forbes-Hamilton and Anna Neagle. Pantomimes are still held here every year. Today the theatre is well known through television: *Sunday Night at the London Palladium*, televised live, was one of the ITV's first great successes. Nearly every international variety star has appeared here, from Judy Garland to Bob Hope.

# Lyric Theatre

Shaftesbury Avenue, W1V 8ES.
Box office telephone: 01-437 3686.
961 seats.

The Lyric opened with a revival of *Dorothy* and it was with money raised from this comic opera that Henry Leslie financed the new theatre. Designed by C. J. Phipps, the building was completed in record time, only ten months, and was ready for the first performance on 17th December 1888. Initially the Lyric staged mainly light opera, with Marie

15

*The facade of the Lyric Theatre with a lyre as the centrepiece of the gable.*

Tempest as the most popular leading lady, although Eleanora Duse, the great Italian actress and rival to Sarah Bernhardt, made her London debut here in *Camille* in 1893 and also appeared in *Fedora* and *The Dolls House*. Bernhardt and Forbes Robertson appeared here in 1902. The theatre has staged a variety of productions. Many revivals were staged under Lewis Waller's control from 1906 to 1910 while during the 1910s and 1920s the theatre was best known for musicals such as *The Chocolate Soldier* (1910) and *Lilac Time* (1922).

A sequence of good humorous and straight plays by contemporary playwrights began and continued throughout the war years. Terence Rattigan's *The Winslow Boy* (1946) was the first post-war success and Roussin's *The Little Hut* (1950) with Robert Morley provided the theatre's longest run of 1261 performances. Successful musicals returned with *Grab me a Gondola* (1956) and *Irma la Douce* (1958), then *Robert and Elizabeth* (1964). Later successes include Alec Guinness in Alan Bennett's *Habeas Corpus* (1970), *John, Paul, George, Ringo . . . and Bert* (1974) and Roger Hall's *Middle Age Spread* (1979).

The auditorium was extensively redecorated in 1933 but much of Phipps' unusual original still remains. Externally the facade to Great Windmill Street is of interest. Now the entrance to dressing rooms, it was built in 1767 as the home of anatomist Dr William Hunter who used it as an anatomical theatre and museum.

# Mayfair Theatre

Stratton Street, W1A 2AN.
Box office telephone: 01-629 3036.
310 seats.

The generous proportions of the Candlelight Ballroom in the Mayfair Hotel made it possible to provide a fully equipped professional stage and just over three hundred comfortable seats when it was converted into the Mayfair Theatre. Since it opened in 1963 with Pirandello's *Six Characters in Search of an Author* starring Ralph Richardson, it has proved a versatile theatre with successes ranging from one-man plays and classical revivals to new plays and musicals. Memorable productions include Christopher Hampton's *The Philanthropist* (1970-3) with Alex McCowen, Aubrey's *Brief Lives* (1970) with Roy Dotrice, Pam Gem's *Dusa, Fish, Stas and Vi* (1977), Gordon Chater in Steve J. Spear's *The Elocution of Benjamin Franklin* (1978) and Richard Harris's *The Business of Murder* (1982).

# Mermaid Theatre

Puddle Dock, Upper Thames Street, EC4V 3DB.
Box office telephone: 01-236 5568.
604 seats.

The original, Elizabethan-style Mermaid Theatre was built in the garden of Bernard

16

Miles's home in St John's Wood and opened in September 1951. In 1953 the theatre was moved to the Royal Exchange for a 13 week season as part of the Coronation celebrations. In 1959 the theatre moved into a renovated warehouse in Puddle Dock and opened with *Lock up Your Daughters,* a rumbustious musical adaptation of Henry Fielding's *Rape upon Rape.* When new office blocks were built on the site in 1978-81 the theatre was incorporated (as a condition for building), and it reopened, enlarged and modernised, in 1981. Bernard Miles set the high production standards which ensured a wide audience for revivals of seventeenth-century plays and works by new authors, commercial hits and plays by foreign authors. The Royal Shakespeare Company's first production when they moved there in 1987 was very much in the original tradition — a rousing production of the *Fair Maid of the West.*

# National Theatre

South Bank, SE1 9PX.
Box office telephone: 01-928 2252.
Olivier, 1160 seats; Lyttelton, 890 seats; Cottesloe, 400 seats.

The National Theatre is three theatres in one complex on the South Bank of the Thames. Largest, with a thrusting stage, is the **Olivier** named after the National's first artistic

director (1962-73), Sir Laurence Olivier. The proscenium-arched **Lyttelton** is named after the first chairman (1962-71) Oliver Lyttelton and the **Cottesloe,** smallest and most adaptable of the three auditoria, is named after Lord Cottesloe, first chairman of the South Bank Board (1962-77).

A national theatre was first proposed in 1848 by a London publisher Effingham Wilson but the first practical scheme appeared in 1904 in the form of a privately printed document, 'A National Theatre Scheme and Estimate'. For over thirty years meetings were held and numerous appeals for money were made. Various sites were proposed, but the project was shelved at the beginning of the Second World War. At last in 1949 under the National Theatre Bill one million pounds was allocated and a building commission was set up under the joint chairmanship of Sir Laurence Olivier and Norman Marshall. Two years later the foundation stone was laid by Princess Elizabeth. In 1962 Sir Laurence Olivier was appointed artistic director of the newly created National Theatre Company which took over the Old Vic as its temporary home until the long-awaited first night in the Lyttelton theatre in March 1976, followed by the Olivier in October and the Cottesloe in March 1977.

Although the massive concrete box-like external structure of the National, designed by Sir Denys Lasdun, one of Britain's leading architects, has been criticised, his excellent use of the internal space, the decor, comfort and

*The National Theatre complex contains the Olivier, the Lyttelton and the Cottesloe theatres.*

congenial atmosphere have been highly praised, as have the excellent productions of classical, new, foreign and experimental plays by the National Theatre Company. Although a relative newcomer to the theatre scene, the National has already developed its own customs and traditions including its very own way of wishing itself good luck on the first night that a play begins, when critics from Britain and abroad are watching. Just before the lights go down and the first lines of the play are spoken, a first night rocket, known as 'Ralph's Rocket', is fired from the theatre's roof. The idea came from Sir Ralph Richardson when the theatre first opened in 1976.

# New London Theatre

Parker Street, WC2B 5PW.
Box office telephone: 01-405 0072.
1106 seats.

If *Cats* ever closes and other productions are staged it will be easier to characterise the New London as a theatre. Its identity concealed behind towering glass walls, the theatre designed by Sean Kenny was perhaps too versatile for its own good until 1982, when Andrew Lloyd Webber exploited an auditorium in which the stage, orchestra pit and front stalls revolve and appropriate walls move. After it opened in 1973 only the opening production, Peter Ustinov's *The Unknown Soldier and His*

*Wife* and the musical *Grease* had any success and during 1977-80 the theatre was used as a television studio. *Cats* opened in 1981.

The Winter Garden Theatre stood on this site until 1965 (it closed in 1959) the last of three previous musical halls there since 1847. It opened as the New Middlesex Theatre of Varieties in 1911 and became a theatre in 1919, presenting musicals with great success, notably *The Vagabond King* with music by Rudolf Friml (1927). One of the last important productions here was *Hotel Paradiso* with Alec Guinness (1956). The theatre closed in 1959 and was demolished in 1965. One of the planning conditions for redevelopment was the building of another theatre on the site.

# Old Vic

Waterloo Road, SE1 8NB.
Box office telephone: 01-928 7616.
1077 seats.

Social reformer Miss Emma Cons bought the Old Vic in 1880 to transform a centre of drunkenness and low entertainment into a temperance music-hall which she called the Royal Victoria Hall and Coffee Tavern. Opened in 1818 as the Royal Coburg (renamed the Royal Victoria in 1833 and nicknamed the Old Vic later) with a good repertoire of melodrama, the theatre had been in decline for many years. Miss Cons's unlikely

*The glass-walled New London Theatre.*

18

*The highly decorated interior of the Palace Theatre — intended to be the home of English opera.*

venture succeeded and in 1898 she was joined by her niece Lilian Baylis, who followed her as manager in 1912. With Miss Baylis's determined and untiring dedication to bringing the best drama to the people at popular prices, the Old Vic became virtually the national centre of Shakespearean production. Between 1915 and 1923 the Old Vic became the first theatre in the world to have staged all thirty-seven of Shakespeare's plays in the First Folio (a feat repeated from 1953 to 1958).

After Miss Baylis acquired Sadler's Wells in 1931 mixed seasons of opera, ballet and drama were put on but without great success. Returning to drama alone, the Old Vic continued to enhance its reputation after Lilian Baylis died in 1937 and following eleven years' closure from 1939 to 1950. The National Theatre Company under Laurence Olivier made it their home from 1963 until the opening of the National Theatre on the South Bank in 1976. After a four year tenure by the Prospect Theatre Company the future of the theatre was in the balance until a Canadian businessman, Ed Murvish, bought it in 1982. He invested in an extensive restoration and modernisation programme and reopened the theatre in October 1983 with Tim Rice's musical *Blondel.*

The brick and stucco exterior and the interior have been restored to their 1880s style and colours. A special feature is a house curtain inlaid with small mirrors which is a replica of the famous 'mirror curtain' of solid glass which was hung in 1822 but taken down for fear that the roof was not strong enough to hold it.

# Palace Theatre

Shaftesbury Avenue, W1V 8AY.
Box office telephone: 01-434 0909.
1450 seats.

Sumptuously decorated and built on a grand scale in 1891, this theatre was built by Richard D'Oyly Carte to be the home of English opera. The first production of Arthur Sullivan's *Ivanhoe* was not a success, there was no home grown product to follow it and after only one year Carte acknowledged defeat and the theatre which opened as the Royal English Opera House became the Palace Theatre of Variety. Offering music-hall very successfully it nevertheless presented more refined entertainments, such as the London debut of the ballerina Pavlova in 1910, which made it a fitting choice for the first Royal Command Variety Show in 1911, in which year Grock made his first appearance in London and the present name was adopted. The first of the musicals which were to be so successful here was *No No Nanette* (1925) and apart from a few straight plays in the 1930s musical entertainment has held the stage ever since. Cicely Courtneidge and Jack Hulbert starred in

Cochrane revues in the 1930s and 1940s and Ivor Novello's *King's Rhapsody* (in which he starred) opened for a long run from 1949 to 1951 when Novello died. All previous records were broken by *The Sound of Music* (1961-7) and again by *Jesus Christ Superstar* (1972-80). Andrew Lloyd Webber's Really Useful Theatre Company bought the theatre in 1983 and since then has had successes with the revival of Rodgers and Hart's *On Your Toes* (1984) and Boublil and Schönberg's *Les Miserables* (1986).

# Phoenix Theatre

Charing Cross Road, WC2H 0JP.
Box office telephone: 01-836 2294.
1012 seats.

With the opening production, in 1930, of Noël Coward's *Private Lives,* starring the author and Gertrude Lawrence, the Phoenix laid the foundations of an almost continuous reputation for intelligent, witty and sophisticated presentations. Designed by Sir Giles

*The Piccadilly Theatre was a cinema for many years.*

*The Phoenix Theatre opened with Noël Coward's 'Private Lives'.*

Gilbert Scott, Bertie Crewe and Cecil Massey, with interior design by Theodore Komisarjevsky, it is a fine example of restrained 1930s taste behind a neo-classical facade. Noël Coward's association with the theatre from its opening was marked in 1969 when the Coward bar was opened just before his seventieth birthday.

Outstanding productions seen here include John Gielgud's revival of Congreve's *Love for Love* (1943), Terence Rattigan's *Playbill* (1948), Paul Scofield's memorable *Hamlet* (1955), John Osborne's *Luther* (1961) with Albert Finney, *The Canterbury Tales* which ran for five years from 1968 and Tom Stoppard's *Night and Day* (1978).

# Piccadilly Theatre

Denman Street, W1V 8DY.
Box office telephone: 01-437 4506.
1170 seats.

Built on the site of derelict stables and opened on 27th April 1928, the Piccadilly was designed by Bertie Crewe and Edward A. Stone. Although built as a theatre, it was taken over as a cinema only four months after opening, showing Britain's first 'talkies' including *The Singing Fool* with Al Jolson.

Nine years later the theatre offered a completely new kind of entertainment when Firth Shepherd presented a continuous programme known as *Choose Your Time* with a newsreel, an orchestra, a Donald Duck cartoon film, variety acts and a short play *Talk of the Devil* with Yvonne Arnaud and John Mills.

The Piccadilly was damaged in the Second World War by flying bombs but soon reopened. The interior was completely redecorated in 1955 and the building reconstructed in 1960 when it became the first London theatre to have air conditioning. Edward Albee's *Who's Afraid of Virginia Woolf* (1964) had its London run here and Henry Fonda made his only West End stage appearance at the Piccadilly in the summer of 1975 in the solo play *Clarence Darrow*. The theatre has staged several Royal Shakespeare Company productions including Pam Gems's *Piaf* (1980) and Willy Russell's *Educating Rita* (1980) which ran for nearly 2000 performances.

# Playhouse Theatre

Northumberland Avenue, WC2N 5DE.
Box office telephone: 01-839 4401.

The Playhouse ceased to function as a live theatre in 1951 when it became a BBC studio until 1975 and was the home for programmes such as *The Goon Show, The Navy Lark* and *Hancock's Half Hour*. It was built in 1882 as the Royal Avenue Theatre but after part of Charing Cross station collapsed on to the building in 1905 the interior was redesigned and rebuilt, opening in 1907 as the Playhouse. Now completely refurbished, with the auditorium faithfully restored to its rich French renaissance style splendour, the theatre reopened in September 1987 with Howard Goodall's new musical *Girlfriends*.

# Prince Edward Theatre

Old Compton Street, W1V 6HS.
Box office telephone: 01-434 8951.
1666 seats.

Opened on 3rd April 1930, the Prince Edward Theatre (named for the then Prince of Wales) was the first of four new theatres opened in London that year (the Cambridge, Phoenix and Whitehall were the others) in what seemed to be the start of a theatrical boom.

The opening musical *Rio Rita* had only a short run, and even though Josephine Baker appeared in 1933 the first five years were so disappointing that the theatre closed in 1935. It reopened in 1936 as a cabaret restaurant named the London Casino and was reputed to take between £6000 and £7000 a week.

From July 1942 it became the Queensbury All Services Club and reopened as a theatre in 1946 with *Pick up Girl*. Lavish musical shows such as *The Dancing Girls*, Robert Nesbit's *Latin Quarter* and Vivian Ellis's *Over the Moon* followed, culminating in *Wish You Were Here* in 1954 for which a swimming pool was built into the stage. In 1954 it was converted into a cinema for *This is Cinerama*. Twenty years later it staged shows again, alternating with film seasons, until Andrew Lloyd Webber and Tim Rice's *Evita* arrived in 1978 and ran until 1986, to be followed by Tim Rice's *Chess*.

# Prince of Wales Theatre

Coventry Street, W1V 8AS.
Box office telephone: 01-839 5987.
1123 seats.

The original theatre here, opened in 1884, was called the Prince's Theatre (renamed in 1886). It was not an immediate success — even Beerbohm Tree in Hawtrey's *The Private Secretary* created little interest — and the first successful production did not arrive until 1891. Two successful musical shows followed. Marie Tempest appeared in several straight plays, in one as Becky Sharp in *Vanity Fair* (1901). Musicals and farces alternated thereafter, followed by revue in the 1930s until 1937 when the building was demolished.

A new theatre opened later in that year with *Les Folies des Londres et Paris*. Designed by Robert Crombie it was ideal for musicals and revues and the comfortable auditorium was cleverly styled to create a theatrical atmosphere and to appear dateless. Sid Field made his London debut here in *Strike a New Note* (1943) and returned to star in *Piccadilly Hayride* (1946). Mary Chase's rabbit *Harvey* was first not seen here in 1949. Later notable productions include Paul Osborn's *The World of Susie Wong* (1959), *Funny Girl* with Barbra Streisand (1966), *Sweet Charity* (1967) and Kurt Weill's *The Threepenny Opera* (1972).

# Purcell Room

South Bank, SE1 8XX.
Box office telephone: 01-928 3191.
370 seats.

Smallest of the three modern concert halls on the South Bank, the Purcell Room is an intimate auditorium. It can seat just over 370 people for a variety of programmes including folk musicians, chamber groups, recitals by solo artists and poetry readings. The foyer, which it shares with the Queen Elizabeth Hall, is used as exhibition space and occasionally for pre-concert entertainment.

# Queen Elizabeth Hall

South Bank, SE1 8XX.
Box office telephone: 01-928 3191.
1000 seats.

With a concert platform boasting thirteen independent sections which can be raised electrically to achieve a variety of tiered levels, the Queen Elizabeth Hall is able to provide a highly adaptable space. Small classical or jazz orchestral concerts, chamber music, ballet and solo recitals are held in the auditorium. Like the Royal Festival Hall and Purcell Room which complete the concert hall trio on the South Bank, the Queen Elizabeth Hall was designed as part of an arts complex which includes the National Film Theatre, the Hayward Gallery and the National Theatre — all connected by high level walkways which provide spectacular views over the river Thames.

# Queen's Theatre

Shaftesbury Avenue, W1V 8BA.
Box office telephone: 01-734 1166.
979 seats.

Named by permission of Queen Alexandra, the Queen's Theatre opened in October 1907. Designed by W. G. R. Sprague as a companion to the Globe (1906) the splendid Edwardian interior, which survived some war dam-

*Masks on the facade of the Queen's Theatre.*

age, being unoccupied for twenty years and rebuilding, is a delightful surprise after the exterior, which did not. Its first success was a musical *The Belle of Britanny* (1908) but its reputation is for successful productions of a wide range of drama. Cecil Hardwicke and Edith Evans appeared in Shaw's *The Apple Cart* in 1929 and John Gielgud made the first of many appearances here in 1930 as Hamlet. Robert Morley's *Short Story* (1935) included in the cast Margaret Rutherford, Marie Tempest, Sybil Thorndike, Rex Harrison and A. E. Matthews. During the run of Daphne du Maurier's *Rebecca* in 1940 the theatre was bombed and did not reopen until 1959, with John Gielgud's solo recital *The Ages of Man*. Vanessa Redgrave made her two appearances in Chekhov's *The Seagull* here (1964, with Peggy Ashcroft, and 1985) and Noël Coward appeared on stage for the last time in his *Suite in Three Keys* in 1966. Alan Bennett's first play here was *Getting On* (1971). Tom Courtenay scored a great success as *The Dresser* by Ronald Harwood (1980) and Julian Mitchell's *Another Country* won the Society of West End Theatres award in 1982.

# Royal Albert Hall

Kensington Gore, SW7 2AT.
Box office telephone: 01-589 8212.
5604 seats.

Solid and monumental, the Royal Albert Hall stands across the road from the highly ornate Albert Memorial, also built in memory of the Prince Consort, Queen Victoria's beloved Albert, but completely different in style. In 1851 Prince Albert had proposed that a

*The Royal Albert Hall.*

'Hall of Arts and Sciences' should be built with the profits from The Great Exhibition but it was only after his death that designs were finally approved and in 1868 Queen Victoria laid the foundation stone. It was during the opening ceremony two years later, that the Bishop of London discovered the famous echo — his 'Amen' was repeated around the hall! Acoustics were greatly improved in 1968, but at one time it was known as the only place in London where a musician could hear his music twice!

The building, with its glass and iron dome, was designed by Captain Fowke and Major-General Scott and inspired by Roman works in Provence. The exterior is painted pink and decorated with a terracotta frieze representing 'The Triumph of Arts and Letters'. A special feature is the Willis organ of nearly 9000 pipes, the largest ever built and once worked by steam engine. The hall has a capacity of 8000 and is used for orchestral, choral and pop concerts, public meetings, balls, sporting events and a host of other entertainments. In 1906, 9000 people crammed into the hall to hear the first gramophone concert and in 1919 the first boxing match was held. Sir Henry Wood's Promenade Concerts were moved here in 1941 and the 'Proms' have been held at the Royal Albert Hall from July to September every year since.

The hall was originally financed by selling seats on a 999 year lease which gave owners free admission to performances. Well over 1000 seats were sold at £100 each — and owners took great pride in their seats. In the 1890s, for example, the heyday of charity balls at the Royal Albert Hall, two sisters had a special trapdoor cut in the dance floor so they could reach their seats without missing out on the fun of the dancing! This system of private ownership of seats still continues in a modified form for about eighty events year year.

# Royal Court Theatre

Sloane Square, SW1 8AS.
Box office telephone: 01-730 1745.
397 seats.

The converted chapel which opened in 1870 as the New Chelsea Theatre and became the Belgravia shortly after had no success until Marie Litton took it over in 1871, and changed its name, once again, to the Royal Court. After it was demolished to widen the road, the present theatre in Sloane Square replaced it in 1888 but it was not until Pinero's *Trelawney of the Wells* was staged in 1898 that the new theatre regained popularity. During the outstanding period 1904-7 J. E. Vedrienne and H. Granville-Barker put on a series of plays ranging from Shakespeare to Galsworthy, but thereafter success was only intermittent (Eden

*The Royal Court Theatre is a centre for innovative and controversial productions.*

Phillpott's *Back to Methuselah* in 1924 and Barry Jackson's modern dress productions of *Macbeth* and *Taming of the Shrew* in 1928) until 1932 when the theatre became a cinema.

It reopened as a theatre in 1952 but in spite of Melville's *Airs on a Shoestring* (1954) and Brecht's *The Threepenny Opera* (1956) it was not until after the English Stage Company took over in 1956 that the Royal Court assumed its continuing role as the centre of innovative and controversial theatre. John Osborne's *Look Back in Anger* (1958) was followed by plays by other new and unconventional authors such as Arnold Wesker, John Arden, Edward Bond, Charles Wood and Mary O'Malley. David Storey's *Home* with John Gielgud and Ralph Richardson (1969) was an outstanding success. Visiting companies such as the Edinburgh Traverse Theatre have also been very successful here.

## Royal Festival Hall

South Bank, SE1 8XX.
Box office telephone: 01-928 3191.
2895 seats.

The Royal Festival Hall was built for the Festival of Britain in 1951 and is owned, maintained and managed by the South Bank Board. It shares a number of facilities with the Purcell Room and the Queen Elizabeth Hall, including a boiler house, which has been used

as a film set for *Dr Who*, and a fire-sprinkler system which is able to shower some 7000 gallons of water. Safety was an important factor in the design of this large hall capable of seating, on vibrant red leather seats, almost 3000 people and which stages about 450 musical events every year. The elm-panelled auditorium is dominated by magnificent sham organ pipes: the real ones — all 7000 of them — are hidden away out of sight. In May 1986 thirty-five years of music at the Festival Hall were celebrated with a weekend of music and amusements from free lunch-time concerts on the Riverside Terrace to a spectacular 4½-hour concert in the hall.

## Royal Opera House, Covent Garden

Bow Street, WC2E 7QA.
Box office telephone: 01-240 1066.
2098 seats.

The name Covent Garden derives from the medieval 40 acre walled garden of the monks of Westminster Abbey. There were three previous theatres on the site before Sir Edward Barry designed the present Royal Opera House in 1858. The Theatre Royal opened in 1732 and was the most luxurious in London. Peg Woffington scandalised London by appearing as a man in Farquhar's *The Constant*

24

*Couple* in 1740 and Garrick appeared here. Oliver Goldsmith's *She Stoops to Conquer* (1773) and Richard Brinsley Sheridan's *The Rivals* (1775) were first staged here. Henry Holland reconstructed the whole interior in 1792. Haydn's 'Creation' had its first performance here in 1800 and John Kemble and Sarah Siddons appeared in 1803.

Because of the high cost of rebuilding (by Smirke) after a fire in 1808 the Shilling Gallery was abolished, causing the Old Price Riots which forced the management to restore it. Between 1809 and 1847 most of the famous actors of the day appeared, including Grimaldi, Macready, Fanny Kemble and Keen. The theatre began to fail after 1842; it closed and reopened as The Royal Italian Opera House in 1847. After another fire in 1856 Sir Edward Barry designed the present neo-classical building which has since been devoted mainly to opera and ballet. It was renamed the Royal Opera House in 1939.

The present auditorium and the mirror-lined crush bar, in rich red and gold, are as grand as befits an international opera house and the necessary extensions and improvements backstage began in July 1982 with the building of rehearsal studios and dressing rooms. When the old proscenium curtains were renewed a few years ago the management had the old ones cut into tiny pieces and made into paperweights which were then sold in aid of the development fund.

# Sadler's Wells Theatre

Rosebery Avenue, EC1R 4TN.
Box office telephone: 01-278 8916.
1499 seats.

By 1683 Richard Sadler had opened a 'Musick House' here and when he found natural wells on his property he added taking the water to the attractions, first brewing it into beer. He renamed his grounds 'Sadler's New Tunbridge Wells' and it was a great success. Since then there has been a virtually unbroken programme of entertainment at Sadler's Wells.

Thomas Rosoman built the first brick theatre in 1765 and Joey Grimaldi, the legendary clown, made the first of many appearances here in 1770 — at the age of two. In 1802 Thomas Dibden exploited the proximity of the New River (dug in 1764) to build a large tank under the stage and fill it with water for aqua shows which included naval battles with large model ships firing real cannon. Under Samuel Phelps, from 1844 to 1862, productions became more serious — he presented all but three of Shakespeare's plays — and audiences and actors were made to behave with decorum in the theatre. After his departure the theatre declined and was used as a music hall (Marie Lloyd and Harry Champion both appeared here), a roller-skating rink, an early cinema but not, as was once suggested before it closed

*The Royal Festival Hall was part of the complex built for the 1951 Festival of Britain.*

down in 1916, as a pickle factory.

Sadler's Wells was exactly what Lilian Baylis was looking for in north London to repeat her success at the Old Vic. By 1926 she had launched an appeal to buy and rebuild the theatre, which reopened on 6th January 1931 with *Twelfth Night*, followed by *Carmen*. Soon it became exclusively the home of opera and ballet (under Ninette de Valois). The excellence of the companies here led to the ballet company moving to Covent Garden in 1945 (it became the Royal Ballet Company in 1956) and the opera company moving to the Coliseum in 1968 to become the English National Opera Company in 1974. The companies formed to take their place are today the Sadler's Wells Ballet Company and the New Sadler's Wells Opera Company.

# St Martin's Theatre

West Street, WC2H 9NH.
Box office telephone: 01-836 1443.
550 seats.

The St Martin's was designed by W. G. R. Sprague in 1913 as a companion to its neighbour the Ambassadors but building work was postponed by the outbreak of war. It finally opened on 23rd November 1916 with *Houp*

*An art-deco urn in the Savoy Theatre.*

STALLS          DRESS
                CIRCLE

*La!*, a musical comedy. In 1920 Alec Rea and Basil Dean took over joint management from C. B. Cochran. Among their first productions was Clemence Dane's *A Bill of Divorcement* (1921). This starred actress Meggie Albanesi who died two years later aged only 23. A memorial plaque with her portrait in bas-relief hangs in the foyer.

The theatre has changed hands many times over the years and has staged a variety of plays, including J. B. Priestley's *When We are Married* (1938), Edward Percy's *The Shop at Sly Corner* (1945), *Penny Plain* (1951) with Joyce Grenfell, and Peter Shaffer's *Sleuth* (1970-3). In 1974 Agatha Christie's *The Mousetrap* transferred here from the Ambassadors to continue its record-breaking run. The architectural style of the theatre is described as 'English Georgian' with classically simple interior decoration, a contrast to the rich extravagance of Victorian theatres.

# Savoy Theatre

Strand, WC2R 0ET.
Box office telephone: 01-836 8888.
1122 seats.

The Savoy was built by Richard D'Oyly Carte especially to stage Gilbert and Sullivan comic operas. Designed by C. J. Phipps it opened in 1881 with *Patience* and made history as the first public building in London to be lit by electricity. A queuing system was introduced to control the disorderly customers for the pit and the gallery. Until 1896 the Savoy Operas, as they came to be known, were regularly produced. When Gilbert and Sullivan finally parted in 1896 other musical shows were put on, including Edward German's *Merrie England* in 1901. The successful record continued from 1907 when Harley Granville-Barker began to stage straight plays, including Shaw's *Caesar and Cleopatra* (1907) and Shakespeare. The children's play *Where The Rainbow Ends* was first seen here in 1911.

The theatre was reconstructed in 1929 by Frank Tugwell and the art-deco design of the interior by Basil Ionides continues to delight audiences today. The new theatre opened with a season of Gilbert and Sullivan, the first for twenty years and extremely popular, and it continued to be a consistently successful house. Notable productions include Kaufman and Hart's *The Man Who Came to Dinner* (1941) Noël Coward's *Sail Away* (1962), *The Secretary Bird* (1968) which, with nearly 1500 performances was the theatre's longest run, Agatha Christie's *Murder At The Vicarage* (1975) and Michael Frayn's *Noises Off* (1982).

# Shaftesbury Theatre

Shaftesbury Avenue, WC2H 8DP.
Box office telephone: 01-379 5399.
1348 seats.

Opened in 1911 this was the last new theatre to be built in Shaftesbury Avenue. It was called the Prince's Theatre and opened on Boxing Day with *The Three Musketeers*. The flamboyant neo-classical interior, designed by Bertie Crewe, appropriately complemented the melodramas on the stage, although the impressive alabaster and gold mosaic ceiling has long been lost. Productions have ranged from plays to ballet and musicals and for forty years it regularly presented the D'Oyly Carte Company in Gilbert and Sullivan operas. *Pal Joey* (1954) and *Wonderful Town* (1955) were successes of the 1950s but in the 1960s the theatre was sold several times and in 1963 the name was changed to the Shaftesbury.

On the day after censorship ended in September 1968, the musical *Hair* opened and caused a sensation because of its nude scene. Its run here (1997 performances) came to an abrupt end when the ceiling collapsed in 1973. The theatre was saved from demolition and placed on the list of Buildings of Special Architectural or Historical Interest in 1974 but its theatrical future remained uncertain until the Theatre of Comedy Company founded by Ray Cooney with the support of some thirty leading theatre personalities leased (in 1983) and then bought the Shaftesbury in 1984. Stephen Sondheim's *Follies* opened in 1987.

# Strand Theatre

Aldwych, WC2B 5LD.
Box office telephone: 01-836 2660.
937 seats.

Built on the site of an earlier theatre, Punch's Playhouse, the Strand opened in May 1905 as the Waldorf. It was built as part of the grand Aldwych/Kingsway plan and designed, by W. G. R. Sprague, together with the Aldwych Theatre to complement the French chateau style of his Waldorf Hotel, completed in 1907. It became the Strand in 1909 (with a short spell as the Whitney from 1911 to 1913). Ivor Novello lived in a flat above the theatre from 1913 to 1951.

Under Louis Meyer in 1912-16 the theatre began to succeed and when Arthur Bourchier took control in 1919 there were several out-standing productions including the first London production of Eugene O'Neill's *Anna Christie* (1923) and Ian Hay's *A Safety Match* (1921). Successes in the 1930s were mainly comedies or farces such as Sellar and Yeat-

man's *1066 and All That* (1935) and Ben Travers's *Banana Ridge* (1938). Donald Wolfit performed Shakespeare at lunchtime during the blitz in 1940 until the theatre was blasted. It reopened quickly and in 1942 began a resounding success with Kesselring's *Arsenic and Old Lace* (1337 performances).

In 1955 *Sailor Beware* made Peggy Mount a star overnight and ran for 1231 performances and the revue *For Adults Only* (1958) was a great success. In complete contrast were C. P. Snow's *The Affair* (1961) and *The New Men* (1962). Frankie Howerd and Robertson Hare starred in *A Funny Thing Happened on the way to the Forum* from 1963 to 1965. In June 1971 *No Sex Please, We're British!* opened to poor reviews and a phenomenal run until 1982 when it transferred to the Garrick where it ran until 1987.

# Theatre Royal, Drury Lane

Catherine Street, WC2E 7QA.
Box office telephone: 01-836 8108.
2283 seats.

There have been four theatres on this site since the first opened in 1663 with Beaumont and Fletcher's *The Humorous Lieutenant*. Nell

*Augustus Harris, whose devotion to Drury Lane earned him the nickname 'Augustus Druriolanus'. He enlivened (critics said 'vulgarised') traditional pantomime with music-hall turns and knockabout comics.*

*The imposing Theatre Royal, Haymarket.*

Gwynne appeared in Dryden's *The Indian Queen* in 1665. The theatre burnt down in 1672 and was replaced by an enormous building attributed to Sir Christopher Wren and opened in 1674. Garrick made his first appearance here in 1742 and in 1747 took over, reformed the management and direction and brought its first period of continuous success. Mrs Siddons made her debut here in 1775 and in 1776 Richard Brinsley Sheridan took over. *School for Scandal* (1777) and all his later plays were produced here. In 1794 he rebuilt an even larger theatre which burned down in 1809. Samuel Whitbread, founder of the brewery, raised the money for a new building, the present theatre by Benjamin Wyatt, which opened in 1812. Edmund Kean made his first appearance here as Shylock in 1814. Grimaldi made his last appearance in 1826.

Never a successful theatre, it declined steadily until 1879 when a series of popular melodramas, pantomimes and spectaculars revived its fortunes. Dan Leno first appeared in 1889, in 1905 Henry Irving played his final season here and Ellen Terry celebrated her jubilee. Forbes-Robertson made his farewell appearance in 1913. Since 1924 Drury Lane has presented many of the great musicals, most of them highly successful and including *Rose Marie* (1925), *Show Boat* (1928), Ivor Novello's productions of his own musicals in the 1930s and Rodgers and Hammerstein shows after the Second World War. *My Fair Lady* ran for 2281 performances from 1958. *A Chorus Line* and *42nd Street* were successes of the 1980s.

There are many busts in the public rooms of people who have been associated with the theatre. Among the most important are those of Dan Leno, Samuel Whitbread and Sir Johnston Forbes-Robertson, the great tragedian. One of the theatre's unique traditions is the Twelfth Night Cake: on his death in 1794 actor Robert Baddeley left money to provide a cake and wine for the green room every year on Twelfth Night. Drury Lane also has its own phantom, the 'Man in Grey', who is said to haunt the Upper Circle, especially during matinees. It is believed to be the ghost of a man whose bones were found behind a wall in 1840.

# Theatre Royal, Haymarket

Haymarket, SW1Y 4HT.
Box office telephone: 01-930 9832.
906 seats.

The Little Theatre in the Hay opened in 1720 but for the first forty years it had no royal patent to present plays and could open only by subterfuge. Nonetheless it was Henry Fielding's ferocious lampoons on the government

28

and the royal family which led to the censorship of plays by the Lord Chamberlain, introduced in 1737 and not repealed until 1968. It was licensed and became a Theatre Royal at last in 1766, although performances were limited to the summer months when Covent Garden and Drury Lane were closed.

The best actors of the day such as Fanny Kemble and John Bannister appeared here and one play *The Tailors* drew such great attention in 1805 that tailors rioted in protest at its satire. A new theatre designed by John Nash was built in 1821 of which the magnificent six-column portico still remains. By the time the great John Buckstone took over in 1853 the Haymarket was the leading playhouse in London. He was a favourite of Queen Victoria and it is his ghost which is said to return to the theatre. He brought E. A. Sothern from the United States to appear as Lord Dundreary (of the whiskers) in *Our American Cousin* (1861). Under the Bancrofts the interior was remodelled by C. J. Phipps with the first picture-frame stage in London (although removing the pit caused a riot on the opening night). Under Beerbohm Tree's management, Oscar Wilde's *A Woman of No Importance* (1893) and *An Ideal Husband* (1895) were first performed, but his greatest success was George du Maurier's *Trilby* (1895) with Tree as Svengali. The interior as it is today was designed by C. Stanley Peach in 1905.

Throughout the twentieth century the Haymarket has had a reputation for outstanding productions of works by contemporary playwrights as well as from the classical repertoire. Most of the celebrated actors of any day have appeared here. Marie Tempest starred in St John Ervine's *The First Mrs Fraser* (1929) and Helen Hayes made her first London appearance in Tennessee Williams's *The Glass Menagerie* in 1948. Enid Bagnold's *The Chalk Garden* was seen in 1956 and Robert Bolt's *The Flowering Cherry* in 1957. Alec Guinness appeared as T. E. Lawrence in *Ross* in 1960 and in John Mortimer's *A Voyage Round my Father* in 1971.

# Vaudeville Theatre

Strand, WC2R 0NH.
Box office telephone: 01-836 9987.
694 seats.

A theatre much bigger than the present one opened in April 1870 with a comedy called *For Love or Money* and in spite of its name, the Vaudeville has mainly presented a varied range of light drama and comedies. Within the first five years it had enormous success

with H. J. Byron's *Our Boys* which ran for 1362 performances (1875-8). Reconstruction in 1891 reduced the seating capacity and the present neo-Georgian facade was added. The first performances in England of Ibsen's *Rosmersholm* and *Hedda Gabler* were given at matinées here in 1891. Seymour Hicks appeared as *Scrooge* in 1901 and his *Bluebell in Fairyland* was revived annually for some years. Gladys Cooper made her West End debut in 1906. For over twenty years from 1915 the theatre presented revues, closing at the end of 1925 for a brief period for reconstruction which produced today's comfortable and elegant interior.

Among many successes were the wartime production of Esther McCracken's *No Medals* (1944), William Douglas Home's *The Chiltern Hundreds* (1947) and Arnold Wesker's *Chips with Everything* (1962). Previous records were broken with *Salad Days* (1954, 2329 performances) by Dorothy Reynolds and Julian Slade. More recent successes include Joyce Rayburn's *The Man Most Likely To* (1968-70) followed by John Chapman and Ray Cooney's *Move Over Mrs Markham* (1970), Agatha Christie's *A Murder is Announced* (1977) and Michael Frayn's award-winning *Benefactors* (1985).

# Victoria Palace Theatre

Victoria Street, SW1E 5EA.
Box office telephone: 01-834 1317.
1565 seats.

Built in 1911 as a variety theatre, the Victoria Palace has continued to stage variety shows throughout most of its history. In 1934 a change to melodrama was attempted and *Young England* by Walter Reynolds was staged but the audience, accustomed to all the fun of variety, would not take the play seriously and came only to laugh and jeer. Special bouncers had to be employed to throw out the over-exuberant, although everyone enjoyed it and the show ran for six months. Widely considered to be one of the best examples of the boisterous era of the music hall, the theatre was designed by Frank Matcham for Alfred Butt and opened on 6th November 1911. The classical facade, faced with white patent stone and decorated with statues, has remained unchanged since then. However, the gilded metal figure of the ballerina Pavlova, a protegée of Butt, which once stood on the tower, was taken down for safety during the Blitz and disappeared. Pavlova apparently had never looked at the statue: she was so superstitious that she would draw the car blinds every time she passed it.

One of the most successful productions here was Lupino Lane's *Me and My Girl* which began in 1937 and ran for over a thousand performances until the outbreak of the Second World War. After the war, the Crazy Gang took over until their farewell in 1962 when it became the home of the Black and White Minstrels for the next eight years. Since then shows have included the musicals *Annie* and *Barnum*.

# Westminster Theatre

Palace Street, SW1E 5JB.
Box office telephone: 01-834 0283.
600 seats.

The building which today houses the Westminster Theatre was originally a chapel, converted in 1924 into a cinema called the St James's Picture Theatre. After further alterations to adapt the crypt into dressing rooms and a bar the building opened as the Westminster Theatre in 1931. During the 1930s and 1940s it established a reputation for staging serious plays by modern playwrights such as Shaw, Ibsen, Granville-Barker, Denis Johnson, Eugene O'Neill and T. S. Eliot. Paul Scofield made his debut in O'Neill's *Desire under the Elms* (1940), Flora Robson starred in James Parrish's *Message for Margaret* (1946) and Lesley Storm's *Black Chiffon* (1949). From 1946 until recently the theatre was run by the Westminster Memorial Trust (whose rare productions promoted the message of Moral Rearmament) for commercial production companies.

# Whitehall Theatre

Whitehall, SW1A 2DY.
Box office telephone: 01-930 7765.
620 seats.

The tall tower-like facade with elongated windows of the Whitehall brought a great deal of favourable comment when the theatre was built in 1930. The clear, well-defined lines of the building designed by Edward A. Stone were so markedly different from the others in Whitehall that one architect commented that it made them look as though they needed a shave. The theatre has from the beginning presented revues, farces and comedies, and opened with Walter Hackett's comedy *The Way to Treat a Woman*. In 1942 the 'Whitehall Follies' were launched, featuring the notorious Phyllis Dixey, the West End's first stripper. Her shows proved so successful that she took over the lease of the theatre until 1947. From 1950 to 1967 the theatre became known

nationally as the home of British farce under the management of Brian Rix. He appeared in most of the 'Whitehall farces' starting with *Reluctant Heroes* (1950). Many of them were televised.

In the 1970s impresario Paul Raymond bought the theatre and brought nudity back to the Whitehall with *Pyjama Tops* (1969-75, 2298 performances) starring Fiona Richmond. Subsequent productions included John Wells's *Anyone for Denis?* (1981). For a short time in the early 1980s the Whitehall became an exhibition hall for a collection, mounted by Raymond, of memorabilia from the two world wars. However, this proved to be against the licensing laws of the theatre and it reopened with live entertainment in 1985.

# Wigmore Hall

Wigmore Street, W1.
Box office telephone: 01-935 2141.
540 seats.

Originally known as Bechstein Hall, this concert hall was built for the German piano manufacturer Friedrich William Bechstein next to his London studios. It opened in 1901, exactly 75 years after his birth, with two invitation concerts. The hall is designed to create an atmosphere intimate enough for chamber music and vocal and instrumental recitals. The dimensions — it is 72 feet (30m) long, 41 feet (12.4m) wide and 32 feet (9.7m) high — were planned to provide the excellent acoustics.

Arthur Rubinstein gave his first piano recital here in May 1912 when he was 25 years old. Critics found him rather too exuberant, but audiences and musicians adored him. After a number of charity concerts during the First World War the hall was closed in 1916 when Bechstein's entire business plus some 137 pianofortes were auctioned for a mere £56,500. The hall alone had cost £100,000 to build. However, it was reopened in 1917 as the Wigmore Hall with a programme of Beethoven's violin and piano sonatas played by Albert Sammons and Vassily Safonoff. Solomon, Hoffmann, Backhaus, Prokofiev and many others played here. In 1940 the young Australian pianist Noel Mewton-Wood made her debut. She killed herself in 1953 and a chair in the artistes' room has an inscription to her memory.

One of the most striking features of the Wigmore Hall is the famous cupola, arched with Numidian marble, over the platform. The painting symbolises the striving of humanity after the great voice of nature. The central

*The cupola of the Wigmore Hall — the Soul of Music lifts his hands to the Genius of Harmony.*

figure is the Soul of Music, whose arms are lifted and whose gaze is directed up to the Genius of Harmony — a ball of eternal fire with rays reflected around the world.

# Wyndham's Theatre

Charing Cross Road, WC2H 0DA.
Box office telephone: 01-836 3028.
760 seats.

Actor/manager Charles Wyndham saw the fulfilment of a dream when he produced the opening play, a revival of *David Garrick,* on 16th November 1899 at Wyndham's, his own theatre. Designed by W. G. R. Sprague, it was built on a site acquired from the Marquess of Salisbury on condition that only Wyndham could build a theatre there. Among the early productions was *An Englishman's Home* in 1909. Described as 'a play by a patriot', the author was soon found to be Gerald du Maurier's soldier brother, Guy. The play, which urged people to listen to Lord Roberts's appeals for awareness that Britain was in grave national danger, not only played to full houses for six months but also attracted a lot of new recruits to the Territorial Army. Tallulah Bankhead made her London debut here in 1924. From 1926 to 1932 seven plays by Edgar Wallace were produced at Wyndham's. The last, *The Green Pack,* was staged the day before his death. Among the most controversial was *Smoky Cell* (1930) with players enacting an electrocution in an American prison.

Important new productions in the 1950s were Peter Ustinov's *The Love of Four Colonels,* Graham Greene's *The Living Room* and one of the longest running successes at the theatre, Sandy Wilson's *The Boyfriend* which opened in 1954 and ran for 2078 performances.

The interior of the theatre has been well preserved and retains the elaborate Louis XVI decorative style. One of the most striking features is the proscenium, set in cream and gold bordering, which forms a complete picture frame. Above are framed portraits of Sheridan and Goldsmith and allegorical figures. The bust in the centre of these figures looks remarkably like Mary Moore, Wyndham's wife. The curtain was replaced in the late 1960s and is an exact replica of the original festooned house curtain.

# FURTHER READING

Arundell, Dennis. *The Story of Sadler's Wells*. David and Charles, 1978.
Billington, Michael. *The Guinness Book of Theatre Facts and Feats*. Guinness Super-
latives, 1982.
Dobbs, Brian. *Drury Lane*. Cassell and Company, 1972.
Elsom, John, and Tomalin, Nicholas. *The History of the National Theatre*. Jonathan Cape, 1978.
Findlater, Richard (editor). *At The Royal Court*. Amber Press, 1981.
Findlater, Richard. *Lilian Baylis — the Lady of the Old Vic*. Allen Lane, 1975.
Glasstone, Victor. *The London Coliseum*. Chadwyk Healy, 1980.
Glasstone, Victor. *Victorian and Edwardian Theatres*. Thames and Hudson, 1975.
Hartnoll, Phyllis. *The Oxford Companion to the Theatre*. Oxford University Press, 1983.
Hawkins, Frank. *The Story of Two Thousand Concerts*. South Place Ethical Society.
Howard, Diana. *London Theatres and Music Halls 1850-1950*. The Library Association, 1970.
Leacroft, Richard. *The Development of the English Playhouse*. Eyre Methuen, 1973.
McCarthy, Sean. *The Old Vic Refurbished*. The Old Vic, 1983.
Mackintosh, Iain, and Sell, Michael (editors). *Curtains!!! Or A New Life for Old Theatres*. John
Offord (Publications), 1982.
Mander, Raymond, and Mitchenson, Joe. *The Lost Theatres of London*. New English Library,
1975.
Mander, Raymond, and Mitchenson, Joe. *The Theatres of London*. New English Library, 1975.
Pope, Walter James Macqueen. *Haymarket, Theatre of Perfection*. W. H. Allen, 1948.
Pope, Walter James Macqueen. *The Melodies Linger On: The Story of the Music Hall*. W. H.
Allen, 1950.
Pope, Walter James Macqueen. *Pillars of Drury Lane*. Hutchinson, 1955.
Roberts, Peter. *The Old Vic Story — A Nation's Theatre*. W. H. Allen, 1976.
Rosenthal, Harold. *Two Centuries of Opera at Covent Garden*. Putnam, 1958.
Roose-Evans, James. *London Theatre*, Phaidon, 1977.
Shawe-Taylor, Desmond. *Covent Garden*. Parish, 1948.
Southern, Richard. *The Victorian Theatre — A Pictorial Survey*. David and Charles, 1970.
Thomas, Peter. *Shakespeare's Theatre*. Routledge and Kegan, 1983.

# PLACES TO VISIT

The theatres listed below offer regular guided tours.

*Barbican Centre*, Silk Street, EC2Y 8DS. Telephone: 01-638 3351.
*National Theatre*, South Bank, SE1 9PX. Telephone: 01-633 0880.
*Old Vic*, Waterloo Road, SE1 8NB. Telephone: 01-328 7558.
*Royal Festival Hall*, South Bank SE1 8XX. Telephone: 01-928 3191.
*Royal Opera House*, Bow Street, Covent Garden, WC2E 7QA. Telephone: 01-240 1200.
*Sadler's Wells Theatre*, Rosebery Avenue, EC1R 4TN. Telephone: 01-278 6563.
*Theatre Royal, Drury Lane*, Catherine Street, WC2E 7QA. Telephone: 01-836 8108.

MUSEUMS

*Shakespeare Globe Museum*, Bear Gardens, Bankside, SE1 9EB. Telephone: 01-928 6342. There
is a model of the original Elizabethan Globe theatre on show. Special events are held
throughout the year and there are regular performances in the theatre, in which there is an
authentic replica of the Cockpit Theatre stage built in 1616.
*Theatre Museum*, 1E Tavistock Street, Covent Garden, WC2E 7PA. (Entrance in Russell Street.)
Telephone: 01-836 7891. One of the richest collections in the world relating to the performing
arts, displayed to show their history and diversity. There are lectures, audio-visual
presentations and some performances in the small theatre.